Concise Guide to the Everest Base Camp Trek: How to Prepare, What to Take and What to Expect

By Katherine Rock

Copyright © Katherine Rock, 2020
First published 2020
ISBN: 979-8-6110-5217-4

**Concise Guide to the Everest Base Camp Trek:
How to Prepare, What to Take and What to Expect**

All rights reserved. Without limiting the rights under copyright reserved above, no part of this publication may be reproduced, stored in or introduced into a database and retrieval system or transmitted in any form or any means (electronic, mechanical, photocopying, recording or otherwise) without the prior written permission of the owner of copyright. All photos are the author's own.

Dedication

To Dad and Dan,

Thank you for your endless support and encouragement.

Contents

Introduction 1

Preparing For The Trek 3

Itinerary 7

Luxury vs Standard Trekking 11

Practical Matters 17

Costs 23

Staying Healthy on Trek 29

Packing List 37

Photography 47

Trip Diary 49

Further Reading 77

Introduction

When I was 16 years old a representative from World Expeditions gave a speech at my school about organising a school trip to Everest Base Camp. That trip didn't go ahead but the idea obviously stuck. In November 2010 (12 years later), after what should have been months of comprehensive physical preparation, I attempted the Everest Base Camp trek. Except my mother had died suddenly 4 months prior to the trip, throwing my training plan into disarray. I should have cancelled the trip but I thought it would cheer me up and give me something to look forward to. I went ahead with the trip but my travelling companion felt ill at Tengboche so we descended to a lower altitude and took an easier walk through the Himalaya. No Kala Pattar or Everest Base Camp for us.

For the following 8 years the fact that I hadn't made it to my goal continued to gnaw at me. I decided for and against a second attempt at the Everest Base Camp trek more times than I can count (or care to admit). Out of the blue the idea struck me to just do the damn thing and be done with it.

I wish I could say why the idea of leaving my comfortable home with my warm bed, hot shower, clean drinking water and ample oxygen to go walking up and down and up a dusty trail at high altitude to sleep in lodges with paper thin walls and shower once-weekly instead of twice-daily appealed. Many people complain of fatigue, gastrointestinal upsets, altitude sickness, boredom, cold, and just wondering what the hell they were thinking. And those are the people who enjoy it. The people who really hate it describe it as a living nightmare. There is no good reason whatsoever for me to do this trek but the idea is irresistible. As naturalist John Muir put it so eloquently "The mountains are calling and I must go".

This time I decided to leave nothing to chance and committed myself to a 'luxury' lodge trek. I rationalised that warm beds, hot showers and good food would do wonders for my energy levels and health, thus improving my chances of successfully reaching base camp. I chose Himalayan Glacier because their tour dates fit in with my schedule but there are several other companies that also offer a luxury option.

I've put together this book to help anyone planning the trek to be ready physically and psychologically for the challenge you're about to undertake. I've covered how to prepare physically for the trip, a typical itinerary, the difference between luxury and standard treks, some advice on practical matters like visas and insurance, an estimate of what you can expect to spend, advice on staying healthy while trekking, and a detailed packing list, including advice on photography gear. I've also included my trip diary so you can see what it was really like, day by day, not just the way I want to remember it.

If you have any questions, please send them to me through my website:

https://www.katseyetravelphotos.com/contact

Preparing for The Trek

Am I fit enough to trek to Everest Base Camp?
The trek to Everest Base Camp is extremely challenging. You need to be in good physical shape in order to enjoy the experience and to succeed in reaching base camp. Some itineraries and guidebooks recommend you start preparing 5 to 6 months in advance. This will depend on your current level of fitness. If you are already fit and active then you may not require this much preparation time. It is crucial to be in good physical shape before you go. You cannot use the walk itself as a shortcut to getting fit.

I started my preparation 3 months prior to my trip. I knew if I started 6 months prior I would lose momentum and probably have to start all over again anyway. It is a personal choice. You need to do as much preparation as it takes for you to feel confident to trek all day, every day, for around 10 to 12 days with lots of uphill and downhill while wearing a small pack (if you have a porter) or a very large pack (if you don't). You will hear the phrase "Nepali flat" a lot on the trek to base camp. It means lots of up and down.

My training largely consisted of gym visits around 3 times a week for 30 minutes of cardio including short bursts of high intensity and around 20 minutes of weights along with bushwalks on most weekends. The walks started short, on flat ground and built up over time to longer walks with more up and down.

Concise Guide to the Everest Base Camp Trek:
How to Prepare, What to Take and What to Expect

3 months before my trek I prepared a training plan. I had a list of walks gradually ascending in length and difficulty. I didn't follow it at all. Sometimes other things came up or it was too hot and I didn't want to risk getting heatstroke. Don't stress too much if your preparation doesn't go exactly according to plan. The important thing is to be fit and healthy and in the habit of walking a lot.

When the weather was too poor for bushwalking I did a couple of stair sessions where I put on my boots and went up and down the 11 flights of stairs in my apartment building over and over and over. This was partly to break in my boots but also to really give my calf muscles a workout and get used to going up and down constantly.

I had planned to do the Wentworth Pass walk in the Blue Mountains, west of Sydney, because it's the same walk Lincoln Hall did as part of his preparation for his 2nd summit attempt on Everest. Sadly the track was closed in the months leading up to my trek.

In addition to being good physical preparation, bushwalking will also give you the chance to test out all your gear in a similar setting in which you'll use it. This is your opportunity to decide what you really need to carry with you all day, such as camera equipment.

Am I too old to trek to Everest Base Camp? Am I too young?

My guide reported his youngest client was an 11-year-old boy and the oldest was 75 years of age. I was 36 when I did the trek and from what I saw, I would say there were more people older than I was than younger on the trail, although not all were going to Everest Base Camp. The oldest person to summit Everest was 80 years of age, so if you are in good health there should be no reason you can't make it to base camp with adequate preparation. Please note that some tour companies have minimum age limits, so make sure you check this in advance. Intrepid for example have a minimum age of 15.

Do I need mountaineering experience to reach Everest Base Camp?

No. There is no climbing required to reach Everest base camp. You will not need to use ropes or ice axes or crampons. It is just walking. Lots and lots of walking.

Concise Guide to the Everest Base Camp Trek:
How to Prepare, What to Take and What to Expect

Itinerary

Most tour groups follow a fairly standard 14-day itinerary, arriving in Kathmandu then flying to Lukla to the start of the trek. In June 2019, the Civil Aviation Authority of Nepal issued a notice that all flights to Lukla during the trekking season would need to depart from Ramechhap airport instead of Kathmandu. There have been mixed reports about whether this has been enforced with some reporting individual trekkers have been allowed to fly from Kathmandu to Lukla but trekking companies have not. If you are travelling independently you will need to re-confirm your travel arrangements shortly before you are due to fly out. If you are travelling with a group be prepared that there may be some changes to your planned itinerary. You may also like to allow extra time in your itinerary in case of flight delays or other issues. Ramechhap is around 4 to 5 hours drive from Kathmandu.

Lukla airport (officially Tenzing–Hillary Airport) is considered by many to be the most dangerous airport in the world. It was built under Hillary's supervision in 1964. In his autobiography, he recounts being unhappy with the top surface of the airfield which he thought was too soft. His solution was to buy a large quantity of chang (locally brewed alcohol) and then hire fifty Sherpas to perform a traditional Sherpa dance featuring much foot-stomping back and forth across the field for two days.

Lukla has the world's shortest take off and landing strip. As you approach the runway it looks like it is set vertically into the mountain. It's either the most exciting or terrifying part of the journey, depending on how you feel about flying. I loved it!

If you really hate the idea of small planes or very short runways, your other option is to take a bus or hire car to Jiri (also known as Giri) and start the walk there. This will add extra time to your journey, for both the bus journey and the additional trekking distance. Personally I found the travelling on Nepal's highways to be pretty hair-raising, so I'm not confident this option would be any less scary.

This is a summary of my itinerary provided by the tour company. It is typical of most organised tours. The time in brackets is the estimated walking time. I typically took much longer!

Day	Activity	Altitude - metres	Altitude - feet
1	Arrival in Kathmandu	1,300	4,265
2	Kathmandu: Sightseeing and trek preparation Buy/rent equipment	1,300	4,265
3	Fly Kathmandu to Lukla Trek Lukla to Phakding (3 to 4 hours)	2,652	8,700
4	Trek Phakding to Namche Bazaar (5 to 6 hours)	3,440	11,286
5	Namche Bazaar acclimatisation day	3,440	11,286
6	Trek Namche Bazaar to Deboche (5 to 6 hours)	3,820	12,533
7	Trek Deboche to	4,360	14,304

Concise Guide to the Everest Base Camp Trek:
How to Prepare, What to Take and What to Expect

Day	Activity	Altitude - metres	Altitude - feet
	Dingboche (4 to 5 hours)		
8	Trek Dingboche to Duglha (3 to 4 hours)	4,600	p15,092
9	Trek Duglha to Lobuche (2 to 3 hours)	4,940	16,207
10	Trek Lobuche to Gorak Shep, visit Everest Base Camp, return to Gorak Shep (6 to 7 hours)	5,364 (Base camp) 5,170 (Gorak Shep)	17,598 (Base camp) 16,962 (Gorak Shep)
11	Trek Gorak Shep to Pheriche, option to visit Kala Patthar (8 to 9 hours)	4,280	14,042
12	Trek Pheriche to Pangboche, Tengboche, Namche Bazaar (6 to 7 hours)	3,440	11,286
13	Trek Namche Bazaar to Lukla (6 hours)	2,800	9,186
14	Fly Lukla to Kathmandu	1,300	4,265
15	Final departure		

Other options

If you're travelling independently and able to choose your own itinerary, I would consider a rest day at Gorak Shep after reaching Everest Base Camp. I was not in the mood to walk anywhere after that exciting but challenging day. The downside of course is that it could be bitterly cold and there's not a lot of entertainment. I would also break up the walk between Namche Bazaar to Lukla on the return journey. The official national park signs estimate this as 10 hours of walking, which I think is too much for one day after 10 continuous days of walking. You could stop at Phakding or Monjo. Both have luxury lodges which would make nice rest stops.

You can book many of the accommodation options online, including the luxury lodges of Yeti Mountain Homes.

I would still use the services of a guide and porter. This is a good way of supporting the local economy for a relatively modest amount of money. My friends who travelled independently had a very precise allocation of wet wipes per person per day for cleaning. You will be sacrificing a lot of comforts if you take the independent option.

Luxury vs Standard Trekking

Should I pay the extra money for a bit of luxury?
This is not an easy question to answer. The trek to Everest Base Camp (EBC) is already expensive if you book through a tour company. It gets very expensive to choose the luxury option. I travelled with Himalayan Glacier. Their standard option is US$2550 per person twin share. Their luxury option is now US$3220 per person twin share, or an additional US$670.

The two most important things to remember are that luxury is a relative term, and the higher up you go, the less luxury there is to be had.

In Phakding, the luxury option will get you a very nice room at Yeti Mountain Home. Rooms feature a private bathroom with hot shower and electric blankets on the beds.

Twin room at Yeti Mountain Home in Phakding

Some rooms have views of the river. There is a large heated dining hall providing excellent, freshly prepared food.

In Namche Bazaar, the luxury option will get you a very nice room at Yeti Mountain Home. My room had a private bathroom with a hot shower and both beds had electric blankets.

Twin room at Yeti Mountain Home in Namche Bazaar

The bar had a happy hour every night where they provided complimentary rum punch and popcorn. The bar is decorated with fascinating photos of the early climbers of the region.

The bar at Yeti Mountain Home in Namche Bazaar

The food in the restaurant was amazing and included traditional Tibetan food or an extensive buffet. Breakfast was made to order and also excellent quality. The only downside of staying here is that to get the great views, the lodge is high up within Namche. It's great once you're there, but it means extra walking on your arrival day, which is already one of the hardest days of the trip.

Sadly, there are no Yeti Mountain Homes in Tengboche. Even on the 'luxury' tour you will stay at the main lodge, although my guide did manage to get me a room with a view of the monastery. The rooms are basic and the bathrooms are shared. There is a large heated dining hall. The food is still good but not nearly as impressive as at the earlier lodges.

Twin room in Tengboche

    The lodges in the smaller villages of Dingboche, Duglha and Lobuche are all very basic. The rooms are cold, there are no electric blankets and the bathrooms are shared. The food is still quite good but not nearly as good as at the luxury teahouses. I once heard teahouse trekking described as "indoor camping" and that description is very apt here. It is quite rustic.

    There is nothing luxurious about the lodge at Gorak Shep. Nothing at all. There is apparently an electric blanket, but the construction of the building was so rough I didn't risk turning it on. The wires were coming out of the walls and I believe that's toilet paper plugging a hole in the window recess.

Single room in Gorak Shep

One of my fondest memories of the trek was arriving at the lodge at Lukla on the return journey, knowing I had virtually completed the trek and could finally rest and relax. I had developed a very severe case of the Khumbu cough which improved enormously after my celebratory hot shower. I enjoyed a delicious cooked chicken breast with fresh salad and slept like a baby in a king-size bed with an electric blanket.

Yeti Mountain Home in Lukla

A higher standard of accommodation and food is really the only difference between a luxury trek and a standard teahouse trek. The guides and porters available will be the same and they all follow a fairly standard 14 or 15-day itinerary.

The verdict?

Totally worth it! The trek is gruelling and I felt so much better rested and more energised from having hot showers on occasion, sleeping warmly and eating well. I had no issues with stomach bugs, I suspect largely because of the very high quality food provided, as well as my guide being able to recommend which foods to eat and which to avoid. I am very glad I paid the extra money for the extra comfort.

Practical Matters

Visa

All foreign nationals, except Indians, need a valid visa to visit Nepal. Visitors from most countries can get a visa on arrival in Nepal. Nationals of the following countries will need to acquire a visa prior to arriving in Nepal: Nigeria, Ghana, Zimbabwe, Swaziland, Cameroon, Somalia, Liberia, Ethiopia, Iraq, Palestine, Afghanistan, Syria.

Refer to the Nepal Department of Immigration website for additional details:

http://www.nepalimmigration.gov.np/page/tourist-visa

I strongly recommend applying for a visa online before arriving in Kathmandu. I didn't do this for my trip. Instead I used the visa kiosks available on arrival at Kathmandu Airport. Only half the kiosks were working and it was a slow process. After filling out the online form at the kiosk you then need to join a second queue to pay the fee. Then there's a third queue to get it all inspected by the customs official. It took a very long time.

Here is the link for the online visa form:

http://online.nepalimmigration.gov.np/tourist-visa

The form should be completed within 15 days prior to your arrival in Nepal.

A tourist visa will cost US$25 for 15 days or US$40 for 30 days. Even if you plan to stay in Nepal for less than 15 days you should probably pay extra to get the 30-day visa. Flights to and from Lukla are often delayed or cancelled which can add extra time to your trip.

You may need exact money for your visa if you are arriving at a land border. If you arrive in Nepal at Kathmandu airport this is not a requirement. You can get change but it will be in Nepali rupee. Major currencies are accepted.

Insurance

You will need insurance that covers you for high altitude trekking at altitudes above 5000 metres (16,404 ft) and emergency evacuation. Make sure you read the fine print. I used World Nomads and the prices are very reasonable. I paid US$70 for my standard policy premium and an extra US$74 to be covered for trekking at altitude (listed on the policy as "Adventure Activities (Level 3) Hiking - up to 6,000 metres").

Make sure you have several copies of your insurance details handy. I suggest a copy in your day pack, a copy in your duffel bag and give a copy to your tour company. Email a copy of all your important documents to yourself so you can access them from any computer.

If you plan to do any climbing while in Nepal (such as Island Peak, which is a popular introduction to mountaineering and can be combined with the Everest Base Camp trek) you will need additional insurance that specifically covers you for this.

Flights

Most treks to Everest Base Camp start from Lukla. It's best to aim for an early morning flight to Lukla if you're booking your own transport. Flights into and out of Lukla are often delayed. My flight to Lukla was scheduled for 6am and finally departed around 10am. Friends of mine were on an 8:30am scheduled flight that was delayed so many times and eventually cancelled. They finally left Kathmandu at 4pm by helicopter. They then had to walk from Lukla to Phakding in the dark.

The departures board at Kathmandu showing flight delays to Lukla

Water

I bought enough water purification tablets for the entire trek but my guide recommended bottled water at some points because the mineral content can cause upset stomachs even after purification. There is now a recycling program in the area so at least the plastic bottles are no longer being burned. Alternatively you can pay for boiled water or take a water sterilisation pen.

Photography

I got the most use out of my mid-range lens and wide-angle lens and relatively little use of my long-range zoom. Refer to the section on photography on page 47 for more detailed recommendations.

Toilets

Toilets are frequent on the trail and are often in surprisingly good condition, but almost none have toilet paper so you'll need to take your own. If you're using a toilet attached to a teahouse be sure to buy something or leave a donation. The odds of making it to EBC and back without using a squat toilet are almost zero, so make sure you know what you are doing. There are online tutorials that can explain the process if this is your first time.

When to go?

Autumn and spring are the popular times on the Everest Base camp trail. Autumn tends to have clear skies which makes for great views. Spring is a little warmer and base camp will actually be in use by climbers. Trekking in winter is an option although it is less popular. Friends of mine have done it. They were snowed in for a few days at one of the smaller lodges. If that's your idea of adventure then go for it. If you're on very tight timelines then a winter trek is probably not a good idea. Summer is the monsoon season and the trail can get muddy and slippery. Leeches can also be a problem. The trail is a lot less popular at this time so it might suit you if you're after some solitude while trekking.

Travelling alone or with a guide and porter

If you decide to trek to EBC without joining a tour you will need to decide whether to travel alone or to hire a guide and/or porter. The path to Everest Base Camp is very well-travelled and popular, particularly in Autumn and Spring. The trail is well marked. You will not need a guide to give you directions and prevent you from getting lost. There are however many other benefits of travelling with a guide. They will give you an idea of what to expect, which days are hardest and help you engage with the culture. They can recommend restaurants, tea houses, call ahead and make bookings and provide medical support and supervision. I was very glad to have my guide to look out for me.

Porter

It is obviously a personal choice whether or not to use the services of a porter, but I believe it is a relatively small amount of money to provide much needed and appreciated employment for someone.

Trail Etiquette and Safety

I was amazed at the speed I saw some people travelling up and down the trail, particularly when they had huge loads on their backs. Always give way to anyone moving faster than you are.

Yaks are commonly used in the Himalaya to transport goods and sometimes ill or injured trekkers. They are very large animals and can easily knock you over or off the side of a mountain. Always stay on the high side of the track when yaks are passing. Do not try to cross a suspension bridge if yaks are approaching from either direction.

Costs

Listed below are the costs of the big-ticket items and new items I bought for the trip. Prices were current at November 2018. The exchange rate has been calculated in January 2020. I already had almost all the gear I needed so I didn't need to spend a lot extra. In total, I spent around US$4,800 dollars (or AUD $6,900) for this trip. Your total trip cost will vary considerably depending on whether you travel independently or on a tour, if you choose a luxury tour and if you need to buy or rent much equipment.

Upfront costs	Cost $US	Cost $AUD	Notes
Luxury Trek	2880	4141	A 25% deposit was required upfront, with the remainder due on arrival in Nepal. The cost has changed since my trip in November 2018. It is now US$3220 if booking through Himalayan Glacier. There are plenty of tour operators such as Intrepid Travel offering

Upfront costs	Cost $US	Cost $AUD	Notes
			standard EBC treks from around US$1200. Many of the cheaper tour options do <u>not</u> include food so you will need to budget extra for this. See the section below for additional information on the cost of food on the trail.
Single supplement	980	1409	This only applies to the hotel in Kathmandu and luxury lodges at lower altitudes. It is a very high price to pay, but is it really luxury if you have to share your room with a stranger? I think not.
Flights	747	1074	Return economy flights from Sydney to Kathmandu with Cathay Pacific booked around 3 months in advance.

Concise Guide to the Everest Base Camp Trek: How to Prepare, What to Take and What to Expect

Medical	Cost $US	Cost $AUD	Notes
Doctor's appointment	60	86	
Diamox	9	13	Price is for 10 tablets. The standard dose is ½ tablet twice per day.
Anti-biotics	15	22	Price is for 1 course.
Hydralyte	13	19	This is the price for the bulk buy pack of 6 tubes of 10 tablets.
Handwarmers	10	14	I have icy cold hands of death so I took 2 packs of 5 pairs of hand warmers at $7 per pack. You can get these from large pharmacies like Chemist Warehouse.
Body warmers	7	10	Price is for 5 body warmers.

Concise Guide to the Everest Base Camp Trek:
How to Prepare, What to Take and What to Expect

Equipment	Cost $US	Cost $AUD	Notes
Head torch	25	36	Usual retail price is $60.
Trekking Poles	15	22	I bought mine in Kathmandu.
Sunglasses	34	49	A pair that fit very close to your head will help keep dust out as well as protecting your eyes.

Here is a summary showing how much of a cost difference it makes to travel on a standard tour instead of a luxury tour. All prices are US dollars.

Expense	Luxury	Standard
Tour	$3220	$1200
Single supplement	$980	Not available
Meals on trek	Included in total price	US$60 per day x 12 days on trek = US$720
Total	$4200	$1920

You would spend around half as much on the trek (including meals) if you were to travel on a standard tour without a single supplement compared to taking the luxury option. I have used the prices quoted on Intrepid.com in January 2020 as a guide. The US$60 per day for meals sounds quite generous when you look at the prices I've listed below but food does get more expensive the higher up you go, particularly for things like snacks and drinks. Some people have reported paying US$10 for a can of pringles. I saw small blocks of Cadbury chocolate selling for around US$7 and that was in Namche where there is plenty of competition.

How much does food cost on the trek?

As of January 2020, 1 US dollar is worth around 115 Nepalese Rupees (NPR).

Tea was typically 100 NPR per cup but I did pay 120 NPR on occasion.

Lunch of steamed momos or noodles with chicken or vegetables and egg and cheese was usually around 500 to 600 NPR.

A litre of water was 200 NPR.

To fully charge a battery in Duglha cost 500 NPR.

I paid 1400 NPR for my snacks in Kathmandu. You can also buy some along the way but they will be more expensive the higher up you go.

I paid 300 NPR for a SIM in Kathmandu and another 1000 NPR for 5GB of mobile data.

If you're travelling independently, a lodge room in Namche will set you back around 200 NPR plus 500 NPR if you want a hot shower. A room with a private bathroom will cost you US$20. Wifi will cost you up to 500 NPR but it is free in some places.

How much should I tip?

For guides and porters the general rule of thumb is to tip around 15% or around a day's pay per week of work. If you book a group tour like I did you won't know how much each person is getting paid. For guides, around US$5 per day is fair. For a porter, around US$2 to

US$4 is fair.

Your porter and guide may not travel back to Kathmandu with you so you should be ready with your tips at the end of your trek before you depart Lukla. You can take currency with you from Kathmandu at the start of your trek or take some cash out on the return journey through Namche.

You should tip your guide and porter in Nepalese Rupee. Tipping is a discreet process in Nepal. You can put your tips in an envelope and pass this to your guide or porter. You may also like to include a card or thank you note. They will probably put the tip away and not open it in front of you.

Where can I get money?

ATMs are readily available in Kathmandu and Namche Bazaar. I recommend getting enough cash in Kathmandu to cover you for the entire trek. You might not feel like exploring Namche in search of an ATM after a hard day's trekking. You also don't want to get caught without cash if the ATMs are not working.

Staying Healthy on Trek

DISCLAIMER: I have no medical training so what follows is purely the result of information I have learned from my own time trekking in Nepal and advice from doctor and guides. You MUST consult a doctor to discuss your trip and your own medical situation.

I recommend seeing a dedicated travel doctor if you can. I did this and my doctor had a very thorough understanding of altitude sickness. She was able to give me very detailed advice including which symptoms would require me to abandon my trip, which symptoms were signs I should take Diamox and when to take it. My doctor reviewed my itinerary to check the rate of ascent per day was reasonable and to confirm enough time was included for acclimatization. Visiting a travel doctor also meant they had all the drugs I needed including Diamox and anti-biotics so I didn't need to make a separate trip to get any prescriptions filled.

The Everest Base Camp trek will take you to some very remote places. It is extremely important you are well prepared to deal with any medical issues that may come up. See your doctor at least 6 weeks before you travel. This will give you enough time to organise any vaccinations you may need and for them to take effect. In addition to any pre-existing medical conditions you may have, you need to be prepared to deal with some common issues on the trail, including altitude sickness, the Khumbu cough, stomach upsets and blisters.

Altitude Sickness
What is altitude sickness?

As you move higher up the mountains, there is less oxygen in the air. As the air becomes 'thinner' it is harder for the human body to function. The effect on the body if the lack of oxygen is termed altitude sickness. At Everest Base Camp, there is around 50% less oxygen in the air than at sea level.

Altitude sickness in its most mild form is also called acute mountain sickness. It is characterised by:
- Headache
- Loss of appetite
- Nausea
- Vomiting
- Tiredness
- Trouble sleeping
- Dizziness
- Shortness of breath during exertion

For most people, these symptoms will resolve by staying at the same altitude and resting. If the symptoms do not go away, it may be necessary to descend to a lower altitude. If you have symptoms of mild altitude sickness/acute mountain sickness, you must not ascend any higher.

In its most severe form, altitude sickness leads to High Altitude Cerebral Oedema (HACE) or fluid on the brain and High Altitude Pulmonary Oedema (HAPE), or fluid on the lungs. HACE and HAPE may occur together. Either HACE and HAPE can be fatal within hours. If you ever feel unwell while trekking you must tell someone immediately.

Symptoms of HACE and HAPE are:
- Confusion
- Shortness of breath while resting
- Frothy sputum (spit)
- Vomiting

When can it occur?

Altitude sickness can occur from 2500 metres (8,000 ft). The airport at Lukla is at an elevation of 2845 metres (9,334 ft). From Day 1 of your trek there is a chance of altitude sickness. Figures vary, but some estimates suggest around 50% of people who travel above 2500 metres will experience acute mountain sickness.

Who will get altitude sickness?

Anyone can suffer from altitude sickness. There's no way of knowing in advance how you will react to high altitude. Some people are susceptible and some are not. And it can vary. Someone that had no problems at high altitude previously can be hit by symptoms very badly at other times. There is a belief that very fit people may be more at risk because they may push themselves to ascend more quickly than less fit people. Ascending more quickly gives them less time to acclimatise.

The only way to prevent altitude sickness is to ascend slowly to give your body time to adjust to the reduced amount of oxygen. If you do have symptoms and they are serious then your only option is to descend to a lower altitude. Don't push yourself thinking this is a once in a lifetime opportunity. The Himalaya will always be there. Don't worry too much if this happens to you. Descending to a lower altitude may not have to mean the end of your trek. On my first attempt to Everest Base Camp, my travelling companion became sick with potential symptoms of altitude sickness. We descended and did an alternative trek at lower altitude. Although it was not the experience I had hoped for, it was still a very enjoyable trek and much less crowded.

On my second attempt I started taking Diamox from the morning of leaving Phakding to go to Namche Bazaar on my guide's instructions. This is earlier than my doctor in Sydney advised me to start, but since my guide has done this trek successfully every year for 30 years I decided to trust his judgement. They are not exaggerating when they say it is a diuretic. The first night I took it I got up 3 times to pee! I was very glad to be in a room with a private bathroom that night. It did settle down after that and I didn't need to visit the bathroom any more often than usual. Make sure you're ready for some night time bathroom breaks when you first start taking it.

Altitude sickness is not something you should ignore. It will not go away on its own. Every day I was in the Himalaya I saw multiple helicopters taking people down to safety. It doesn't only happen to climbers on the mountain. It happens to trekkers much lower down. Take it slowly. Descend if you need to. Tell someone if you feel unwell. The sooner your guide, friends or others know you are unwell, the sooner they can help you and the easier it will be to get you to safety.

For more information about altitude sickness, visit the Travel Doctor website:

https://www.traveldoctor.com.au/healthy-travel-facts/adventure-travel

Staying hydrated is one of the best ways to combat altitude sickness. My doctor recommended taking Hydralyte (oral rehydration solution) during the trek. Rather than consuming it as a standard dose she recommended 1 tablet per litre for all of my drinking water. For every 1 litre of water I drank I first used 1 purification tablet, let that sit for at least 30 minutes as per the instructions, and then added 1 tablet of Hydralyte.

Khumbu Cough

The combination of very dry air at high altitude and cold temperatures can lead to a persistent hacking cough known as the Khumbu cough. I suspect all the dust and dirt kicked up by the trail also contribute to the coughing. This is a common ailment among trekkers to Everest Base Camp. Coughing can get so bad it can lead to torn muscles and broken ribs.

Wearing a face mask or neck mask while walking may help to keep a little moisture in the air as you breathe. Steam from a hot shower can help (if you can find one!). I found breathing in the steam from my tea helped a little too. My cough improved significantly on the return journey once I reached Lukla and had a long hot shower but it took several weeks after I returned home for it to disappear completely.

Food

I recommend eating the local cuisine. My favourites were dal bhat, stir fried noodles, noodle soup and momos. Dal bhat is typically vegetable curry, lentil soup, and white rice. Sometimes there may be a meat curry. It is often served with roti or pappadums. The restaurant or teahouse will top up your meal if you need more of any of the individual dishes. You might hear references to "24-hour dal bhat", or "Dal bhat power 24-hour". There is a thought that dal bhat gives trekkers enough energy to keep going for 24 hours. Momos are a steamed dumpling, typically filled with meat, vegetables or cheese.

It is forbidden to kill animals within Sagarmatha National Park so once you are more than a couple of days into your trek any meat available will be of questionable age and origin. I recommend going vegetarian for the majority of the trek rather than risk getting sick. If you're travelling with a guide they will be able to recommend the safest food options at each location.

You will usually find western options on menus in teahouses, but these are often different to what you would get at home. The teahouses are trying to cater to a lot of different tastes and may not be set up to cook everything the way you are used to. I once ordered macaroni and cheese and received a large plate of macaroni that had been fried in oil, with grated cheese sprinkled on top. Best to stick with the local specialities.

Concise Guide to the Everest Base Camp Trek:
How to Prepare, What to Take and What to Expect

Stir fried noodles

Tibetan Hot Pot

My doctor recommended a probiotic to reduce the risk of stomach upsets, starting from shortly before the trek and continuing throughout the trek. I started taking a daily probiotic from a week before I left and stopped when I returned home. You can get probiotics from the supermarket or chemist that don't require refrigeration which is more convenient when you're trekking.

Blisters

I had worn my boots in for months in advance of the trek but I still had a few small blisters start to form on the second last day. Even if you're very confident about your boots I would still recommend taking something to use for blisters, such as a mixture of regular band-aids and blister plasters. I kept the majority in my big bag and a few in my day pack in case any problems came up while walking.

Concise Guide to the Everest Base Camp Trek:
How to Prepare, What to Take and What to Expect

Packing List

Here is a list of everything I took with me and a few things I wish I had taken. Sometimes I have included the reasons for packing an item, others are self-explanatory. If you're travelling with the support of a porter, they will carry most of your stuff in an expedition or duffel bag. You will carry only your daily essentials while you are walking. Remember that your porter won't walk with you so you won't be able to retrieve anything from the duffel bag until you reach your accommodation for the night. Some tour companies will provide a duffel bag, others will require you to do so. You can buy reasonable quality duffel bags quite cheaply in Kathmandu. Porters are allowed to carry a maximum weight limit of 30 kilograms (around 66 pounds) shared between two trekkers, so you can take up to 15 kilograms (33 pounds) per person.

Clothing
- Boots and spare boot laces

This is one thing you absolutely should not buy in Kathmandu at the start of your trek. You need to buy your boots months in advance so you have adequate time to wear them in. I have a pair of Salomon X-Ultra boots which I have been very happy with.

- Socks

I took 4 pairs of thick hiking socks in colours so bright they must be a safety feature. I wore a few pairs on rotation and kept 1 pair clean for sleeping in.

- Dust mask or neck gaiter

Concise Guide to the Everest Base Camp Trek:
How to Prepare, What to Take and What to Expect

The trail gets very dusty so you will need a face mask or lightweight neck gaiter to avoid breathing in all that dust. There are plenty available for sale in Thamel (the tourist district of Kathmandu) that you wear around your neck and pull up to cover your nose and mouth. I didn't have one on the first trek thinking I could use a bandana tied around my face as a substitute but that did not work at all. It was too thick to breathe through and fell down anyway.

- Down jacket

Many tour companies will loan you a down jacket for the duration of the trek. If not, you can take your own or rent or buy one in Kathmandu. Your tour guide should be able to recommend a reliable shop if you want to rent or buy in Kathmandu. Your down jacket will be one of the most essential items of your trip so it is worth investing in something high quality.

- Fleece jacket

I wore a thick fleece jacket under my down jacket on most days. Once I warmed up from walking I often took off the down jacket and just wore the fleece.

- Rain jacket

If you are travelling with a tour company and they provide a down jacket I suggest waiting to buy a rain jacket in Kathmandu so you can test if it will fit over the down jacket. The rain jacket I packed from home was too small to fit over the bulky down jacket I was loaned so I had to buy a new rain jacket in Kathmandu.

I recommend taking your rain jacket in your day pack to start the trek. I had mine packed in the duffel bag for the flight to Lukla. I could have used it a short time later when it started to rain a little but the porter had already gone on ahead with the duffel bag and my rain jacket.

- Rain pants

I took a cheap pair of rain pants. I did not need them at all but I still recommend taking them. If you get wet and cold you could be in trouble very quickly.

- Beanie

I took my favourite beanie from home but there are plenty of shops in Kathmandu selling beanies.

- Thermal underwear

I took 2 sets of thermals – long sleeve merino wool tops and bottoms. I would wear one top during the day and change into the other one to sleep in. I tried wearing the thermal pants to walk in but I found I went from warm to overheated very quickly. Whether you try walking in thermal pants will depend on personal preferences and the conditions. I recommend changing into clean clothes soon after you arrive at your teahouse. If you wait until bedtime you will have cooled down a lot and won't feel like undressing.

- Trekking pants

I bought mine in Kathmandu. I paid around US$15.

- Gloves

I wore lightweight merino glove liners with warmer gloves on top. That way I could take off the warmer gloves to work the camera but still have some protection against the cold.

- Walking shoes to wear around the teahouses

Some teahouses will provide crocs to wear around the teahouse (with your hiking socks for warmth, stylish!). I took a lightweight pair of runners so I knew I would have a back-up pair of shoes I could still trek in if anything went wrong with my boots.

- Tracksuit pants

These are to wear around the lodges and possibly to sleep in.

- T-shirts
- Underwear
- A clean set of clothes to change into at the end of the trek

It's a wonderful feeling to return to Kathmandu at the end of the trek, have a long hot shower, put on clean clothes and not walk anywhere for a while.

Accessories
- Hydration bladder

One of the best things you can do to limit the effects of high altitude is to stay hydrated. I find the hydration bladder works well because it is easy to sip on constantly and I don't have to stop and fumble for a water bottle. Mine is a 2-litre Kathmandu brand.

- Water bottles – 2 x 1 litre bottles

You will need to enough water bottles to carry 2 or 3 litres of water.

If you are taking a hydration bladder you should also take a water bottle. The hose of the hydration bladder can freeze in the cold at high altitude leaving you without access to your water. Using the bottle is also an easy way to measure the correct amount of water if you're using purification tablets.

- Trekking backpack/Day bag

This is the bag you will carry with you all day (assuming you have a porter carrying everything else). It needs to be large enough to carry your water, snacks, down jacket, camera, money and anything else you may want while trekking. Remember, your porter won't be walking with you so anything you will want during the day has to go in this bag. I took my Kathmandu 'Anabatic' 30 litre hiking pack with cushioned shoulder straps and waist strap.

- Sleeping bag

You will need a four-season down sleeping bag. Many of the tour companies will provide this for you. You can also buy or rent these in Thamel.

- Sleeping bag liner

This is a very small liner you put inside your sleeping bag which adds a little bit of extra warmth. It also reduces the 'yuck' factor if you are sleeping in a borrowed or rented bag.

- Trekking poles

You can buy these in Thamel for around US$15. I did this on both of my treks and the poles lasted the distance.

Concise Guide to the Everest Base Camp Trek:
How to Prepare, What to Take and What to Expect

- Ear plugs

For a little peace and quiet while trying to sleep in the teahouses. All the building materials need to be carried up the mountain so the walls are very thin. The noise from the room above mine in Deboche sounded like another trekker would fall through their floor/my ceiling any minute.

- Hat/Beanie

I took a hat and beanie but it was cold enough that I wore the beanie almost exclusively. If you might do the same you'll need to put on sunscreen every day to protect your skin.

- Sunglasses

These need to be high UV protection. Something that wraps right around your face is ideal to give you protection on all sides.

- Small pocketknife/Swiss army knife

I took mine with me though I never used it. I just felt better to know I could attend to blisters or anything else minor like that.

- Tissues/Handkerchief

The cold air can make noses run and head colds often do the rounds among trekkers.

- At least 2 passport-size photographs

You will need one for your trekking permit. The other is a back-up in case you lose your passport. You may also need one if you buy a SIM card in Nepal, although some stores are able to take a photo for you.

- Headtorch with extra batteries

You will need this in case you are still out walking after dark or to find your way around lodges at night. Just be careful to angle it down when inside so you don't blind your fellow trekkers.

- "Hot hands" body warmers and hand warmers

I used the body warmers to keep me warm at night in bed, although the instructions specifically warn you not to use them while sleeping. It was -14°C (6.8°F) inside. I stand by my choice. They also make toe warmers but these are not designed for use while walking, although you may like to have these to warm your feet while resting at the teahouses.

- Large Ziploc bags

I packed all my stuff into large Ziploc bags to keep everything organised in the duffel bag and to keep it waterproof.

- Small padlock or combination lock

This is more to stop your zippers from working their way open rather than to keep out potential thieves, although this is a possibility.

- Journal and pen
- Sewing kit
- A small roll of electrical tape for emergency repairs

Food

- Energy gels

I experienced a marked loss of appetite at high altitude on the first trek, so I took some energy gels for the second attempt. You can buy these at pharmacies and supermarkets.

- Snacks

Although I experienced some loss of appetite at high altitude I could usually convince myself to eat a chocolate bar when I didn't want to eat a proper meal. There are many western snack foods available in the supermarkets of Thamel, so don't bother flying in to Nepal with a suitcase full of your favourite treats. I recommend buying individually wrapped chocolates. They're easier to throw into the pocket of a jacket or backpack. Large blocks of chocolate can freeze solid and become very difficult to eat in the cold weather.

Concise Guide to the Everest Base Camp Trek:
How to Prepare, What to Take and What to Expect

First Aid Kit

If you're travelling on a tour, your guide will have a first aid kit, but I like to take my own so I have it handy if I need anything. It also takes the pressure off the communal kit. I carried a small amount of bandaids, headache tablets, Diamox and water purification tablets with me in my day pack. Everything else stayed in the duffel pack carried by the porter.

- Altitude sickness tablets (Diamox)
- Anti-biotics
- Antiseptic cream
- Aspirin
- Bandage
- Bandaids
- Cold and flu tablets
- Imodium/Gastrostop
- Hydralyte
- Ibuprofen
- Lozenges
- Panadol
- Steri-strips for blisters
- Safety pins
- Probiotics
- Ural
- Water purification tablets (Aquatabs)

Water tablets taste so much better now than they used to. They no longer have that iodine taste. If you add hydralyte to your water you won't notice the taste either. Alternatively you might prefer to use a purification pen or straw.

Technology

- Kindle and charger
- Phone and charger
- Travel adaptor

Concise Guide to the Everest Base Camp Trek:
How to Prepare, What to Take and What to Expect

Camera Equipment
- Smartphone or Camera, lenses, spare batteries, charger

I took two camera bodies – my Olympus EM10 and EM10 Mark II and my 3 best lenses - M. Zuiko 7-14mm F2.8, 12-40mm F2.8, 40-150mm F2.8 (equivalent in 35mm focal length to 14-28, 24-80 and 80-300 respectively).

I was happy to have all of it but it was a lot to carry. If 3 lenses are too much to carry I used my mid-range zoom (12-40mm / equivalent to 24-80 on 35mm) slightly more than my wide angle lens. I used my long lens the least.

Please refer to the photography section on page 47 for more details.

Toiletries
- Hand sanitiser

The toilets along the trek are really quite reasonable considering their remote location, but you are very unlikely to have soap and water for washing your hands.
- Toilet paper
- Shampoo, conditioner and soap

The luxury lodges will have soap but not much else in the way of toiletries. Other lodges are likely to have nothing at all.
- Dry shampoo

You are likely to go days and days without seeing a shower. So if you have long hair and like me you can't bear the idea of getting it wet in very cold conditions, you may like to take dry shampoo.
- Wet wipes

These will be your "shower" at higher altitude where there are no shower facilities or it's too damn cold to take your clothes off.
- Washcloth for "showering" using bowls of water
- Lip gloss

Use a lipgloss with SPF50 during the day to protect your lips against the sun and Vaseline at night for extra moisture.

- Sunscreen

To protect your skin from the sun at high altitude

- Toothbrush
- Toothpaste
- Floss
- Body lotion
- Brush or comb
- Deodorant
- Nail clippers
- Feminine hygiene products

Documents

I always take printed copies of the following and I also send myself a scanned copy by email in case all my bags go missing:

- ATM card
- Credit card
- Tour booking confirmation
- Flight details
- Insurance information
- Itinerary
- Passport

Photography

What camera should I take with me?

This really depends on whether you are travelling independently or with the support of a porter and on how much you are prepared to carry with you during the day. If you are travelling independently and carrying all of your own gear then size and weight will be major factors.

If you have a porter to carry your expedition bag then you are really only limited by what you are willing to carry with you during the day. Friends of mine were trekking for 2 months in Nepal the same time I was on my way to Everest base camp. They carried all their own gear so they used their smart phones to take photos. They are both experienced and talented photographers and they routinely take great shots on their smart phones. My smart phone photos look like a chimpanzee stole my phone and accidentally took a photo from a moving vehicle.

I have a small Olympus micro 4/3rds mirrorless camera that I love. It's a lot smaller and lighter than a DSLR but still produces great images. Because the camera is light, it only needs a lightweight tripod. I don't believe in spending good money on cameras and lenses and then leaving them at home when I travel because they weigh too much or are too valuable to take overseas!

The only advice I can give you is to test how comfortable you are carrying all your gear on some very long hikes and then decide what you are willing to carry to EBC. Bear in mind that the trail is very dusty and changing lenses during the trek can be risky for getting dust on your sensor.

I took my Olympus with a standard zoom lens (equivalent to 24 to 80 on 35mm), wide angle lens (equivalent to 14 to 24 on 35mm) and long lens (equivalent to 80 to 300 on 35mm). I carried it in a wrap-up water repellent camera cloth within my daypack. My tripod stayed in the expedition bag that was carried by the porter. If you have a porter on your trip they may walk much faster than you do, so anything in your expedition bag may be out of your reach until you arrive at your next camp or teahouse.

Porter's typically have a maximum weight allowance of 30kg, so you need to factor this into your calculations. Although you might start out determined to carry all your gear yourself, at higher altitudes you may need more support, so set aside some of your weight allocation for this purpose.

I packed my tripod and the porter carried it in the expedition bag. It was so cold during the nights and early mornings that I only used my tripod once. I would only recommend packing a tripod if you are confident you will use it. If you only use a tripod very infrequently at home you probably won't need it in Nepal. If you're really worried you might miss out then consider taking something lightweight just for this trip.

Don't forget your usual accessories: tripod plate, cable release, camera cleaning equipment.

Trip Diary

Day 1 – Sydney

It occurred to me while I was waiting in line to drop off my bag at the airport – I'm finally on my way again. After 3 months of preparation, 8 years of waiting to return and even longer of dreaming about it, at last I am on my way to Everest Base Camp. My partner Dan asked me if I'm nervous. I'm not really. I feel I've done everything I can. I didn't do quite as much walking as I would have liked but I do think I've done enough. I think I've packed everything I'm likely to need. I've done plenty of research.

Kathmandu

I left the airport and found my driver waiting with a sign with my name on it. Such a welcome sight after a long day of travel. With him was my guide, Ram. It turns out I am the only person in the tour 'group'. I would have preferred to have other people for company but I will probably meet people along the way.

Day 2 - Kathmandu

I'm so excited I've been jumping around my hotel room. I'm finally going to Everest Base Camp! I bought my trekking poles and trekking pants today. I collected my duffel bag, sleeping bag, map and t-shirt. I'm ready. I'm rearing to go. Let's do it!

I'm feeling well prepared. I had my trip briefing at the tour office today. I had already thought of everything they discussed such as water purification, ascending slowly, taking extra snacks and so on. I've been promised a private room all the way and even the few rooms that don't have en suite bathrooms should have indoor bathrooms at least. Luxury!

I enjoyed an excellent group dinner tonight with some other clients from the same tour company. It was a welcome dinner for me and for Ashleigh, a final year medical student from Melbourne who is doing the Everest Base Camp trek and Island Peak summit along with Manoj from India. Because they'll also be climbing, their itinerary is slightly different to mine and they have their own guide and porter. It was also a farewell dinner for John and Lisa, father and daughter from Switzerland who just completed the Annapurna Base Camp trek. Manoj has met Sherpa Tenzing Norgay which I thought was awesome.

Day 3 - Kathmandu

I had a wonderful day of sightseeing around Kathmandu today. We started at the monkey temple, Swayambhunath. There is a statue of Buddha at the entrance with a wishing well marked 'World Peace'.

My tour guide for today gave me some coins to toss. I got one clean in the centre which he said was good luck and a sign I would make it to Everest Base Camp this time. He also said Ram, my trek guide, had called him last night and told him how anxious he was to make sure I had a successful trip this time.

Next we visited Durbar Square where I was blessed by the Kumari, a very young living goddess, apparently further evidence of my good fortune for the trek.

We visited Boudhanath which was my favourite part of the day. We spent lots of time walking around it, taking photos. We ate lunch at a roof-top restaurant with a great view of the stupa.

Concise Guide to the Everest Base Camp Trek:
How to Prepare, What to Take and What to Expect

Boudhanath Stupa, Kathmandu

After lunch we visited the Hindu temple of Pashupatinath. A funeral pyre was being prepared and two bodies were being prepared for cremation. The place was crawling with monkeys. A particular type of bug flew into my hair which is apparently good luck. It seems all the luck is on my side this time!

I saw several sacred cows wandering on major roads today. Traffic is just as chaotic as I remember it though there doesn't seem to be any aggression in it. Cars seem to nudge their way to wherever they need to go without any apparent rules or etiquette and bikes and scooters pour through the spaces around them.

I met up with some friends for dinner who are spending the next 2 months in Nepal. They are travelling independently and carrying all their own gear. I'm sure it will be wonderful but I think I will have had enough well before 2 months is up.

I had a call from reception to tell me my flight has been changed from 9:00am to 6:15am tomorrow. This is much better. Flights tend to be significantly delayed so an earlier scheduled flight probably means flying a couple of hours later than planned. A flight scheduled for later in the day could get cancelled altogether.

I had caught a cough at the office just before my trip but I decided to push on with the trek anyway. I woke up at 3:30am and had a massive coughing fit and wondered "what the fuck am I doing here?!"

What kind of person spends thousands of dollars to travel so far and walk up and down all day in cold weather to no purpose? Someone with a perverse sense of fun, I guess.

Day 4 – Kathmandu to Lukla and Phakding

How wonderful to be back in the Himalaya again!

True to form all flights were delayed this morning. First our 6am flight was delayed until 7am. Then 8am. Then 8:30 and so on. We eventually departed Kathmandu at around 10am. The flight was amazing! It was such a joy to see the mountains again. It took a second to grasp that they were there because they were so obscured by clouds with just a series of jagged peaks poking out over the top.

The landing was spectacular. I hadn't been able to see the runway from my seat last time but I had a great view today through the cockpit window. The runway looks vertical! These Nepali pilots must have nerves of steel!

Lukla was quite chilly on arrival and I started to worry I was unprepared. I warmed up a lot as we started walking even electing to have lunch outside initially. I gave up on that idea when I realised how quickly my food would cool down. It was a great feeling to finally be on the trail and on my way after so much anticipation. By lunchtime any trace of doubt about what I was doing had evaporated. I feel bad that Dan is alone for a couple of weeks, but I think this is better than me regretting later not taking the chance when I had it. Flying over the Himalaya today I felt loved and supported and free. I can't imagine my life getting any better.

There was a lot more wildlife on the trail than I remembered from last time. Lots of ponies, yaks and even a few people riding horses. I saw two people descending on ponies who appeared to be ill. I saw a third person being carried out on a stretcher.

Our porter looks about 15 years old but apparently he is 24. He arrived at the airport to greet us in thongs. I was very relieved when I saw him later to see he was in walking shoes.

We had a very good dinner tonight. Vegetable soup entrée, dal bhat for the main and chocolate brownie for dessert. I have been coughing so much I am starting to worry I will sprain a muscle or crack a rib. If I couldn't complete the trek because of this damn cough I will be devastated.

I was very glad to read tonight that even Sir Edmund Hillary considered tomorrow's trek from Phakding to Namche 'formidable'. I have done this part of the trek before and it was very challenging.

Day 5 – Phakding to Namche Bazaar

I have arrived in Namche! What a day. Gruelling but very satisfying.

I woke up this morning to the gentle roar of the river flowing. Enjoyed a breakfast of cereal, toast, eggs and tea. Left the lodge around 8am and walked for around 3 hours. I felt much better today after taking some cough medicine my guide gave me. I felt much more confident as a result. The scenery was amazing. We walked by the river for most of the morning. The water is a fantastic colour, like a milky turquoise. The weather was very good. Clear skies for most of the day but then clouding over in the early afternoon.

I was very hungry and a bit tired so I was very glad when Ram turned into a restaurant for lunch. I had milk tea and potato momos for lunch. Carbs wrapped in other carbs. Excellent!

I learned that Ram has two adult children studying in Sydney. He thinks they'll both try to get permanent residency. He says that once young people go overseas they are reluctant to return to Nepal. I'm not surprised. It's a very hard life for most of them. I'm staggered seeing how jovial some of the porters are with the huge loads they carry. I can't help but feel like an incredibly spoiled brat for ever having complained about my 8-hour a day office job.

We had great views of Khumbila today. It's sacred to the Sherpa people and is one of the mountains forbidden to climb. It is the origin of the name for the Khumbu region.

This morning's walking had lots of up and down but no long stretches. It was enough to raise the heartrate though.

There are quite a few helicopters around. Ram says they are mostly for rescues or scenic flights.

I took Ram's advice and started on Diamox this morning. I debated last night about whether I should trust my doctor's extensive training in Sydney or Ram's extensive experience doing this trek. In the end I decided to trust Ram. I also didn't want the trek to be a struggle so I thought it made more sense to start the Diamox early.

I was very glad to be travelling alone when we stopped in Jorsale for lunch today. There were three older English people eating lunch there. They seemed like nice enough people but they kept rabbiting on about how obsessed people are with their mobile phones back home. Travelling alone I can just relax and be present in the moment without other people drawing me away with thoughts of home.

Quite moderate weather today. I walked in trekking pants, t-shirt and fleece for most of the day but I started out with the rain jacket on for extra warmth. I needed the glove liners a couple of times.

After lunch it was another 30 minutes or so of mostly flat walking before we started the climb uphill to Namche. It wasn't too bad to begin with but after a couple of hours uphill it began to seem never-ending. And it's almost all uphill so there's no chance to catch your breath. I took regular short breaks to catch my breath a little but not so long that my muscles cooled down. I was relieved to hear at one of the checkpoints that other people were finding it challenging too. We finally made it to Namche and I was so relieved! I was tired though and started to move slowly and I got cold. I had the feeling I might pass out so I sat and rested for a minute. I continued uphill again until I made it to the lodge. It's a beautiful lodge and has a great view but it really is at the top of Namche.

I feel like a champion for getting to Namche! Ram high fived me when we arrived.

I enjoyed a nice hot shower and made my way to the sitting room. It's nicely appointed with wicker furniture and decorated with lots of photos. There are panoramic views of the amphitheatre that is Namche Bazaar.

I nearly fell asleep in the bar tonight waiting for dinner to be served. It was a hard day. The bar is decorated with photos of Sir Edmund Hillary and Sherpa Tenzing Norgay's successful summit of Everest. Brilliant!

Dinner was excellent. Pea soup entrée, buffet of grilled chicken, roast potatoes, steamed vegetables, pasta, salads and pudding for dessert.

Ram says he is very confident I will reach base camp. This year alone he has escorted a 75-year old man and an 11-year old boy. I am very glad to have Ram as my guide. It's been very reassuring to have someone looking out for me and who can tell me what to expect.

If the weather had been clear today we would have had our first views of Everest. We did see a Himalayan tahr and some mountain goats. The trail was much less busy today than yesterday which was a welcome change.

Day 6 – Namche Bazaar

I woke up to answer the call of nature three times last night. I guess it's a sign the Diamox is working. I had to put on my down jacket to visit the en suite bathroom. I suspect it is just as cold inside the lodge as it is outside. I'm very glad to have a private room so I'm not disturbing someone with my movements and coughing.

There are rows of tents of people camping in Namche. Ram could not make sense of it. 25 years ago it was necessary when there were fewer lodges and the food quality was questionable, but not now. I don't envy them.

Breakfast was porridge, boiled eggs, toast and milk tea. It was biting cold when we left the lodge to go walking this morning. Today is an acclimatisation day. I started to feel ill almost instantly. Then I lost circulation in my toes. I knew it was just the cold weather and once I warmed up from walking I would be fine. Sure enough within a couple of minutes I was OK again. I think knowing what to expect makes a big difference.

We took a short walk to the viewpoint about Namche. It has great views of Everest, Lhotse, Khumbila and partial views of Ama Dabam.

There is also a statue there to honour Sherpa Tenzing Norgay and his ascent of Everest with Sir Edmund Hillary. The statue is on an elevated rock platform, presumably to represent the summit of Everest. But there is also a sign on it which read 'Do not climb'. Oh the irony!

We took a walk around the top of Namche along the old trading route to Tibet. They used to trade salt. Tibet would be about a week's walk from here but the route is closed now. The walk had great views down the valley to the river. We had lunch in the centre of Namche.

I've had a slight headache at brief points throughout the day. I guess it's the altitude. I've had no muscle soreness. My hips were a little stiff when I woke up this morning, probably from carrying my day pack with lots of water and all my camera gear.

I explored Namche a little this afternoon and topped up my snack supplies. Namche was just as I remembered it but even more densely crowded with shops. Prices are much more expensive than in Kathmandu. It should be no surprise. You would have to pay me a small fortune to carry anything up that hill. 100g chocolate bars are selling for around $10 AUD.

Dinner was excellent again. We had Tibetan food tonight. A hot pot of vegetables and meat served over a flame, followed by pork momos, chicken, noodles and chocolate pudding for dessert.

Day 7 – Namche to Tengboche

I'm in Tengboche and I feel fine!

Last time I was here I was feeling tired when I arrived so I didn't explore. First thing the next morning we had to descend because my travelling companion was unwell. This time I feel great and I have plenty of time to explore.

Breakfast was porridge, boiled eggs and coffee. We left around 8am and bumped into Ashleigh and Manoj just above the lodge. Manoj seemed in good spirits but Ashleigh was not well. She has caught a cold and hasn't been eating much. I sympathise. I was the same on my first trip. I didn't sleep well in the teahouses, I had little appetite, didn't eat much and had no energy for walking. Ashleigh and Manoj had an even tougher time getting to Namche. Because they arrived so late from Kathmandu they didn't have time to walk to Phakding on their first day of trekking. They only walked for around 90 minutes from Lukla on their first day so they had an extra 2 hours of walking on their day to Namche. Ram thinks it is unlikely Ashleigh will make it to the summit of Island Peak.

This morning's walk was extremely pleasant. We had great views of Everest and Ama Dablam for most of the walk. The walk was mostly gentle ups and downs so quite easy. Today I can understand why Chris and Julia are here for two months. I could easily see myself coming back again to go to Ama Dablam base camp or the Annapurna circuit. The trail was much wider today and not so many yaks.

We stopped by the river for a lunch of vegetable noodles with cheese and mint tea. The walk after lunch was much more difficult. It was around 2 solid hours of uphill. My calf muscles felt on fire a few times. But I knew it would be easier than the walk to Namche and that helped. I think being prepared psychologically is so important for a trip like this. Knowing what to expect, how to prepare and what to bring has made a huge difference.

I have suffered from trekker's remorse several times already during this trip. There were several times during the long walk up to Namche when I worried I had made a terrible mistake. What had possessed me to fly far from home to trudge uphill in bitter cold past yaks, through yak dung and to no real purpose? To make matters worse, everyone on the trail seemed to be moving faster than I was, even porters with very heavy loads and people at least twice my age. You could call me the tortoise of the Himalaya. But the views get better and better throughout the trek and the walking gets easier.

I'm staying at a standard lodge in Tengboche. There are no luxury lodges here. There is no power in the room to charge batteries, the mattress is thin, the blankets are thin, the curtains are thin, the windows are single pane, the toilet is shared and the water in the taps is frozen. But the views are stunning. I can see the monastery from my bedroom window.

Tengboche Monastery

Poor Ram asked if he could borrow the blanket from the second bed in my room. They must not be giving trekking staff very much for warmth.

Clouds move so rapidly in the mountains. I stopped to take a photo of the mountains and by the time I had taken my lens cap off the mountain had been obscured by clouds.

I slept in my beanie, thermals and track pants last night. Today I started walking in a thermal singlet, t-shirt, fleece and down jacket. I did not need the down jacket for most of the day.

It is bitterly cold tonight. I was swearing as I got changed. I had forgotten to change into my sleeping clothes when we arrived so I had to do it right before bed. It was so cold I swore I would never return to this place. I never want to be this cold again.

Manoj laid down his thoughts on Everest tonight over dinner. He says it's not that difficult a climb, technically speaking. You just need lots of Sherpas and some high altitude training. Ama Dablam is real climbing apparently. This is Manoj's first trip to Nepal so he can't have climbed either. Tonight's conversation made me quite glad to be travelling alone. I think spending all day with other people would be a bit much.

Day 8 - Tengboche to Dingboche

So cold again this morning. I could see the condensation from my breath in the dining room – the only room with heating. I went out this morning to take star trail photos. None of them turned out well but it was still amazing to see a star-filled sky above the Himalaya. I had to unlatch the bolt in the doors of the lodge to get out. There was somebody else already out there with a tripod which made me feel less crazy for being out in the cold and dark on a freezing morning.

Everything was frozen. I was frozen. The ground was frozen. Even the water drum for manually flushing the toilet had huge chunks of ice in it. The air was so cold it felt like it was burning my nose.

We walked in shade for the first 45 minutes or so. It took much longer than usual to warm up. I lost sensation in my toes almost immediately. It started to return after about 20 minutes but it took 45 minutes to return completely. We walked for around 3 hours this morning over mostly flat ground. We had great views of Everest, Lhotse and Ama Dablam. The track was generally wide with some occasional very narrow stretches of only 30 cm or so.

We walked past the site of a landslide. The ground had obviously just crumbled away leaving a semi-circle crater off the cliff edge.

I had a really nice moment on the trek this morning. In addition to enjoying this trip infinitely more than the first, I've already been farther and higher than last time.

We stopped for lunch in Sonam of fried rice and ginger tea. We're at 4000 metres (13,123 ft) now and I feel fine. I'm possibly more out of breath relative the level of exertion than I would usually be but it's hard to say.

I got so hot while walking today I was down to my t-shirt and thermal singlet.

I think the cough I brought from home is almost cured but it's being replaced by the Khumbu cough.

Ram has never had altitude sickness, only a slight headache. He was telling us at breakfast this morning a lot of people don't follow his advice. One professor drank only a half litre of water one day, much less than the 3 litres Ram recommends. The professor told Ram he was seeing double. Ram told him he was very fortunate as most people have to pay twice to see Everest twice!

This afternoon's walk was much easier than I expected. Gentle uphill for the most part. We got to the teahouse around 2pm. We were 90 minutes early for afternoon tea! We're at 4400 metres (14,436 ft) now. My face felt tingly from the Diamox when we first arrived and every so often I feel the threat of a headache but none have ever eventuated. I've had no loss of appetite. I had my usual pre-breakfast biscuits then porridge and tea, fried rice for lunch, pringles and chocolate on arrival at the teahouse, tea and biscuits in the afternoon and Sherpa stew for dinner. For dessert, a pomegranate Ram carried up from Kathmandu. He really has been brilliant.

I'm sitting in the dining room, enjoying the warmth from the stove. It's a smaller teahouse than last night which makes for a much warmer dining room. Ram's had a lot of friends to talk to these last couple of days which is nice to see. It must be dull for him to do the same walk over and over. He is confident I will make it to base camp. I share his optimism. I have no reason to think I will be affected by altitude so it's all looking good.

Day 9 – Dingboche to Duglha

I woke up to another achingly cold morning. I looked out the window to see if there was a view but a thick mist had come in and all was white. On closer inspection I realised the moisture inside the room had frozen on the window. It took me such a long time to psych myself up to leave my sleeping bag. It's not like I was lightly dressed – 2 layers on the bottom, 4 layers on top and a beanie. Packing everything up was painful. Everything felt like ice to touch. I have enjoyed the overall experience immensely but I would not be in a hurry to return.

The walk started out in shade which was hard. The sunlight makes a huge difference. I lost feeling in my toes very quickly and it took around an hour to return. Today's walking was mostly flat through open fields with mountains all around. Brilliant! I saw Pumori and Cho Oyu for the first time.

We bumped into Ashleigh and Manoj shortly after we started. Poor Ashleigh also has a stomach-ache. She did say she was feeling better today and she pushed on to Lobuche after lunch. They are due to reach Everest base camp tomorrow.

The last part of our walk into Duglha was over the moraine which was quite challenging. Lots of the water is still frozen. I had to choose my steps very carefully. I'm still moving very slowly but I don't ever feel like I am struggling.

It's so cold when we first start walking each day that I'm reminded how important psychological preparation is. I know enough to remind myself that I'm just cold and the cold air makes it hard to breathe. I know if I can just keep going for 5 minutes I will be fine. It also helps that I know what to expect in terms of food and accommodation.

Arrived in Duglha around 11:30am after 3 hours of walking. Still no real symptoms of altitude sickness although I did feel more worn out than I would have expected after only 3 hours of walking. I saw someone eating hot chips at lunch so I ordered the same. They were very disappointing. I will stick to Nepali food from now on.

I was supposed to go for a short walk with Ram at 2pm this afternoon. At 2 he knocked on my door and I was still napping. He decided the weather was bad so we skipped it. I had another nap. Then I did as much preparation as I could for tomorrow from under the blankets, including a wet wipe 'shower'. Ram mentioned today that Pheriche, where we'll stop on the way down, is the second coldest place after Gorak Shep. So it's even colder than Tengboche was!

I have put my thermal pants on to wear under my trekking pants tomorrow. I may overheat and regret it but I can't bear the thought of changing pants again in the morning.

I overheard an older English lady at lunch say she had embraced her inner snail for this trek. I like that.

My email to Dan last night hasn't gone through. The battery is almost dead from the cold even though I charged it last night. I won't bother charging it again now because the battery will probably die again before I get reception anyway. I will try again tomorrow. What a difference the right support makes! I've lost count of the number of times I've reminded myself of Dan's words that I have an abundance of determination.

Tonight's lodge is very basic but because I'm on the luxury tour I get special treatment. My room is right next door to the western style toilet and it's been reserved for me.

I wonder how Chris and Julia are going. Two months of trekking, carrying all their own stuff, and the cold! It sounds like punishment to me but they are probably loving it. They're much more hard core than I am.

Oh dear. It's 5:30pm and almost dark and there are people still walking because both of the lodges in Duglha are full.

I have a bit of a headache tonight and it's not going away on its own. I'm also sneezing so I may be getting a cold. Perhaps a cold is better than altitude sickness. I'm very tired and I want to go to bed but I need to use the loo first so my bladder won't wake me in the middle of the night.

The headache didn't go away on its own so I took one of Ram's tablets (I think ibuprofen and aspirin) and felt much better soon after.

I slept well once I put my earplugs in. I could hear lots of footsteps above me. It sounded like the ceiling might give way any second and someone would come crashing into my bedroom.

I felt very glad not to be going to Lobuche today like Ashleigh and Manoj. With a headache already plus an altitude gain of another 300 metres (984 ft) followed by base camp the next day would have been too much for me. Even if I had been successful in getting to base camp I don't think I would have enjoyed the experience.

Day 10 – Duglha to Lobuche

I woke up this morning toasty and warm and even a little overheated. I did have 4 layers of clothing on and 2 blankets doubled over to make 4. It was slightly less bitterly cold this morning. I woke up and it occurred to me that if all continues to go well I will be at Everest Base Camp tomorrow!

We walked to Lobuche quite quickly this morning in around an hour and 40 minutes. It was slow progress, especially to begin with. I get out of breath very quickly, especially on the uphill sections. We are now at an altitude of 5000 metres (16,404). I had a slight headache but it passed on its own.

We walked up (of course!) to the top of a nearby hill for great views of the Khumbu glacier and distant views of base camp. I'm going to make it!

I went out to take photos this afternoon but I didn't last long. I felt like my nostrils were burning again and I worried I would get a nosebleed.

Yaks in Lobuche

Had a restful afternoon.

I heard from Ram that Ashleigh needed a horse to get from Gorak Shep to Everest base camp. I doubted the wisdom of continuing on if she needed a horse but she did seem determined. Ram seems unimpressed at their itinerary. Apparently two guides have died here in the last week. I lost count of the number of helicopters we saw today.

Today we passed through the memorial to the climbers who have died on Everest. It stretches over a large area and is a very sobering sight.

Day 11 – Lobuche to Everest Base Camp to Gorak Shep
I did it! I did it! I did it!
I made it to Everest Base Camp today.

I woke up this morning and thought 'today is the day!'. It's finally happening. I waved my arms around like an excited kid.

I thought it had been even colder than usual last night. I learned at breakfast it had been -4°C (25°F) overnight in the bedrooms. The guide for one of the large groups told them whoever was ready should wait outside for the others. No-one moved. I was chatting to an older Canadian man while we warmed our hands at the stove waiting for breakfast to be served. He shared my sentiments. It's been an incredible experience but I wouldn't do it again.

The walk from Lobuche to Gorak Shep was very hard work. We started in the shade so it was bitterly cold. I lost feeling in my fingers and it was very painful when it returned. I started to feel unwell but managed to keep going until we reached a sunny patch. I sat down but felt like I might pass out. I shifted position so I was sitting with my back resting against a boulder. I had some water and chocolate and felt well enough to continue. It was hard work going over the moraine. There were some parts where it was hard to get past other people which made me think of the stories of traffic jams amongst Everest climbers.

I still needed to make a decision on whether to go up Kala Patthar. Ram made it very clear he would happily take me if I wanted to go but he also had some reservations he wanted me to understand. It would be a 4:30am start, so very early, cold and dark. The track is very steep and slippery. The view is not much better than the views we see anyway. He also thought I would be tired after the trek to base camp.

We made good time to Gorak Shep, under 2 hours, I think. Ashleigh and Manoj were there having breakfast. I asked their opinion of Kala Patthar. Ashleigh had got about half way up and turned back. She said it was painfully cold and she worried about getting frostbite or frostnip. She also said it was a goat track. Manoj went all the way. He said it was too cold to even work the camera and he only managed to take one picture. He claimed it was worth it but he looked absolutely shattered. I decided against going up Kala Patthar. I'm sure the views are very good but there have been so many stunning views already. There must be plenty of amazing places to visit in the Himalaya but I don't have the capacity or the interest to visit every single one. Getting up early to scramble up a goat track in the freezing cold sounds like punishment to me.

We left Gorak Shep around 10:30am after a very early lunch. I felt very emotional to finally be so close. I got all teary. I was moving slowly because of the altitude but otherwise I felt fine. I felt nothing could stop me. I took a photo of the iconic 'Way to Everest BC' sign. Soon after we started walking I told Ram my decision to skip Kala Patthar. He suggested we walk tomorrow all the way down to Pangboche instead of Pheriche as originally planned, thus skipping the second coldest stop on our itinerary. While he was on the phone booking the lodge in Pangboche I walked ahead, knowing he would catch up to me very easily. There was no-one ahead of me on the trail so I felt like I had the walk to base camp all to myself. Such an amazing feeling. The excitement! The anticipation!

 The track became hard going soon after. Lots of up and down over the moraine, though no really steep sections. I was very tired already and I felt confident I had made the right choice to skip Kala Patthar.

Although it was only a two hour trek to base camp, those two hours really dragged. At times I desperately wanted to sit and rest a while. But Ram maintained a consistent pace. I knew by now to trust his judgement so I kept up with him as best I could. Even though I knew we were so close, the fact that I expected to stumble into base camp any second but didn't somehow made it seem farther away. Eventually the track started to slope down to what I knew must be Everest Base Camp. All I could think was that I had more uphill waiting for me on the return journey. But then – prayer flags and signs. We had made it! Even the usually reserved Ram knew this was no time for a high five. He hugged me and congratulated me on making it to Everest Base Camp! I felt overjoyed. I teared up again. We posed for photos and then I had a few minutes by myself to explore and let it all sink in. A girlhood dream come true. An idea that caught my imagination 20 years ago, first attempted 8 years ago, months of research and preparation and now at last – success!

I took some photos and observed the Khumbu icefall that gives Everest climbers so much trouble. As I was posing for a photo we heard an avalanche on the other side of the glacier.

I tried calling Dan and he tried calling me but the technology didn't cooperate so we didn't get to talk. I think he got the text message so he knows I'm safe and well. Only 6 more days until I'm home again.

Ram started to move me along from base camp. I wanted to linger some more but he was right to do it. The wind started to pick up and it was quite cold. It also made the trail even dustier. The walk back seemed much faster. We celebrated our achievement back at the lodge with milk tea and biscuits.

I feel relieved to know that even if something goes wrong now it won't jeopardise getting to base camp. The walking should get easier from here too. Even though there will still be plenty of up and down the overall trajectory will be down.

I made it. What a wonderful day!

Day 12 – Gorak Shep to Pangboche

Today has been a massive let down after yesterday. I woke up this morning and I thought 'I don't want to walk anywhere'. It's been 8 solid days of walking already. I made it to Everest Base Camp yesterday. Let's crack open a bottle of champagne and take it easy! I didn't sleep well last night. It was cold so it took me a long time to fall asleep. Ram estimates it was around -13°C or -14°C (around 7°F to 9°F) in our rooms last night. That explains why the water was frozen in my hydration bladder tube.

I absolutely hated walking over the moraine today. I was so glad when Ram turned and told me the hardest part was over. We saw a helicopter land in Lobuche to collect some trekkers. I can already feel the change in altitude. I feel like I'm exerting myself less to do the same activities.

We stopped for lunch in Duglha. This cold has finally caught up with me. I had a little nap sitting at the table with my back resting against the wall. Seeing how tired and ill I was Ram tried to hurry me out the door! He got on my nerves all day. At one point he didn't want me to stop and blow my nose because it would take too long. He was weirdly fixated on getting to the lodge on time. We had planned to arrive at 2:30pm but instead we arrived at 3:30pm. It's light until around 5:30 so what's the big deal? We could have stopped for more rests. Maybe even a water break or two. And he is so pushy about medicines! Two days ago he was giving me an expectorant and now he is giving me a cough suppressant. He seems to think I should take every Nepali medicine ever made and then walk for 8 hours as a cure for everything.

I wanted potato and cheese momos for dinner but Ram insisted they're no good here. So I ordered something else for dinner at 6:30pm. At 6:20 Ram came knocking on my door to tell me I had to eat early because I'm their only customer today. So I went immediately to the dining room and when did they serve dinner? 6:30pm! I barely ate my curried vegetables with rice. Ram commented that a lot of trekkers seem to lose their appetites as they come back down from high altitude. I didn't have the heart to tell him it's because we're all so fucking sick of rice!

I am so over it today! I would give anything to be back home with Dan. Poor Dan. I've hardly been able to communicate with him at all this week. I know he will understand but it still must be very lonely for him.

I thought by doing the walk all the way to Pangboche today we would have only a few hours of walking tomorrow but apparently it's another 7 or 8 hours from here to Namche. And I have blisters today for the first time on the trek.

Never again!

Day 13 – Pangboche to Namche Bazaar

I had a very poor night sleep last night because of my coughing. At least it wasn't as cold last night as it had been in Gorak Shep. I still wasn't in the mood to walk but at least I had the promise of contact with Dan and a hot shower to spur me on. We covered the same ground we had been over on the way up. It wasn't a particularly hard day but my feet were sore and I was coughing a lot.

We stopped for lunch at the same restaurant by the river. I can tell now who is going up and who is coming down. The people going up are clean and shiny and full of excitement. I am full of knowledge but no enthusiasm. People going up are so clean they don't need to hide their hair. The people going down are coughing.

There was a young girl, Australian I think, at Gorak Shep who had the quietest, daintiest little cough and would apologise so profusely each time. I think she was affecting a Khumbu cough. She sounded like a Jane Austen character ever so politely clearing her throat in front of the vicar while the rest of us sounded like we had escaped the TB ward for one last hurrah.

We finally made it to Yeti Mountain Home in Namche at 3pm and had a good hot shower, my first in about a week. I shampooed my hair then had a nice long text conversation with Dan. I emailed my Dad to tell him I was safe.

Now I'm enjoying happy hour in the bar except there is an American lady who gives me a death stare every time I cough. Just wait. Your turn is coming!

I had made a joke to Dan earlier that some of the helicopters weren't for rescues but for people like me who just don't want to walk anymore. It turns out an Australian man was killed a few days ago descending from Ama Dablam and another was killed in a rafting trip.

Day 14 – Namche Bazaar to Lukla

I made it! This time I really made it. I had naively thought I had made it once I reached base camp but there was still so much more work to do. 8 days up and 3 days down is a punishing schedule.

I had another shocking night's sleep last night because of the coughing. It took a while to get packed up because I was moving so slowly. Ram even gave me a hard time for being 15 minutes late to breakfast!

We started walking around 7am. It was hard going because I wasn't breathing well. I had no energy because whenever I try to eat it set me off coughing. It was a brutal day on the trail. My feet were so sore. My knees were sore. I was coughing convulsively. The path consisted of so many small rocks which were rough on my already sore feet. My back was getting sore from carrying my camera equipment around. I stopped to let some mules pass and the load of one knocked me a little. Because I was braced so as to not get knocked over the force of the impact made me twist on my knee a little. It hurt at the time but there was no damage done. Still, it put me on edge as a reminder of how badly something like that could turn out. Two other trekkers had moved to the low side of the track to avoid the mules and Ram had to motion to them to move to safety. It would have been a long drop to the valley floor if they had been knocked off. There were a couple of times I went for a little slide on some loose rocks. It was never in a spot that would have ended with me falling off a cliff but it was enough to annoy me when I was already in a foul mood. At one point Ram floated the idea of me riding a horse the rest of the way but I was determined to finish the walk.

We stopped for morning tea but eating biscuits just made me cough. It was the same at lunch. I had noodle soup but the solid food made me cough and I could only drink the broth. I was making a terrible wheezing sound with every breath. It was like my lungs were trying to suck in massive amounts of air but there was dust in my airways. I Googled my symptoms and bronchitis sounds like a real possibility.

The official Sagarmatha National Park signs estimate the walking time from Namche to Lukla at 10 hours. It is too much for one day, especially after 10 continuous days of trekking.

I was so exhausted and sore. Today's walk seemed never-ending. I kept thinking to myself 'any minute now we'll turn a corner and I'll see Lukla' but it never appeared. The trail just seemed to go on and on and up and up. Sometimes I felt like I was walking in an Escher sketch – the stairs just go endlessly up. But then – finally – we walked around a corner and there was Yeti Mountain Home, Lukla! Now I really had finally made it. Of course the lodge is up 6 flights of stairs. I think that is the only downside of the luxury lodge. They put them up high to get the best views.

Ram and I enjoyed our customary tea and biscuits and then I had what was certainly the best hot shower of my life. The steam put some much needed moisture back into my lungs and my breathing improved immeasurably.

Dinner was excellent but sadly I didn't get to eat much of it. The solid food made me cough. Pity. There was a sizzling plate of delicious chicken breast, my first meat in a week or so. And the salad was so good. Just plain lettuce in an oil dressing and well seasoned.

Oh how I have missed salad.

I climbed into my queen size bed with electric blanket and fell asleep, so glad the trek is over.

Day 15 – Lukla

I woke up this morning feeling much better. I still have a slight cough but I'm not wheezing. And I ate breakfast without any coughing fits. I'm at Lukla airport now, waiting for the flight to Kathmandu. I will miss looking out the window and seeing the Himalaya but I am ready to go home. It certainly has been a unique adventure.

Further Reading

This is a list of my favourite books about Everest, Nepal or trekking generally to get you in the mood for your visit.

The Envelope: Walking Up to Everest Base Camp
By Andrew Stevenson
A modern pilgrimage story as Andrew treks to base camp to farewell his late brother. A very insightful account of the local people and full of wry observations on his fellow trekkers.

View from the Summit
By Sir Edmund Hillary
Sir Edmund Hillary's story of the first successful summit of Everest in 1953 with Sherpa Tenzing Norgay. Written in a very down to earth style with some occasional touches of brilliant Kiwi humour.

Trek Everest Base Camp: A survival guide to hiking to the base of the tallest mountain in the world
By Jason Weise and Laura Roberts
Very well-written and comprehensive guidebook to the EBC trek. If you're still deciding whether to travel solo or in a group, with a porter or without, what time of year to go and so on, this book has very detailed and useful information.

Dead Lucky

By Lincoln Hall

Pioneering Australian climber Lincoln Hall was struck with cerebral oedema (fluid on the brain) high on Everest after his successful summit bid in 2006. He was given up for dead and reported as such by the media. He survived a night high on the mountain without shelter and to great surprise lived and safely returned down the mountain.

Into Thin Air

By John Krakauer

A fascinating account of what went wrong during the deadly climbing season of 1996 in which 8 climbers died in a single day on Mount Everest.

A Walk in the Woods

By Bill Bryson

Story of his walk through the Appalachian Trail. Brilliantly funny and a wonderful reminder of the joys of walking. Nothing to do with Everest or Nepal, but great inspiration to throw on your boots and go outside.

Concise Guide to the Everest Base Camp Trek:
How to Prepare, What to Take and What to Expect

Milton Keynes UK
Ingram Content Group UK Ltd.
UKHW012214300823
427775UK00007B/811